Why do Black Women Organise?

A comparative analysis of black women's voluntary sector organisations in Britain and their relationship to the state

Sonia Davis and Veronica Cooke

Policy Studies Institute
London

UNIVERSITY OF WESTMINSTER

PSI is a wholly owned subsidiary of the University of Westminster

The Joseph Rowntree Foundation has supported this project as part of its programme of research and innovative development projects, which it hopes will be of value to policy makers, practitioners and service users. The facts presented and views expressed in this report are, however, those of the authors and not necessarily those of the Foundation.

Published for the Joseph Rowntree Foundation by the Policy Studies Institute.

A CIP catalogue record for this book is available from the British Library.

ISBN 0 85374 800 4
PSI Report No. 885

Typeset by PCS Mapping & DTP, Gateshead
Printed in the United Kingdom by Henry Ling Limited,
at the Dorset Press, Dorchester, DT1 1HD

For further information contact
Policy Studies Institute, 100 Park Village East, London NW1 3SR
Tel: (020) 7468 0468 Fax: (020) 7468 2201 Email: pubs@psi.org.uk
www.psi.org.uk

Contents

Acknowledgements   iv

1. **Introduction**   1
   Aims and objectives   2
   Methods   3

2. **Why Black Women's Organisations?**   5
   Black political identity   5
   Justice and social inclusion   7
   Self-help, autonomy and empowerment   7
   The initial impetus for organisation   9
   Local contexts: generic principles   11

3. **Types and Structures of Black Women's Organisations**   13
   Client groups and services   13
   Male client groups   15
   Structures of organisation   16

4. **Black Women's Organisations and the State**   18
   Local government: strategies and policies   19
   Funding patterns   21
   Funding refugee and migrant organisations   22
   Absence of services for diasporic African women   23
   Levels of funding to black women's organisations   25

5. **Black Women's Organisations in Britain**   30
   Summary of findings   30
   Findings and recommendations   32
   Conclusion   34

Appendices
I   Organisations used as Case Studies   37
II   Organisations in the Local Clusters Survey   38
III Local Authorities Interviewed   40
IV   Funding Bodies Supporting the 14 Case Study Organisations   41

References   42

Acknowledgements

The authors would like to thank all those black women's organisations and individuals who participated in the research, particularly the representatives from the core groups who provided the case studies for the report, and gave us so much of their time and critical analysis. Special thanks to Sandra Jowett at Luton University for her support throughout this project, and also to our research assistant Lisa James for her hard work, good humour and endless cups of tea! Thank you to all the members of the steering committee who offered their advice, support and encouragement. We must also thank all the local authority officers who gave up their time to be interviewed and provided us with much valuable information. Finally, our thanks go to Patricia Davis for her painstaking transcribing of the interviews and focus-group meetings.

1. Introduction

Organisations of black women in Britain could with some justification be described as hidden from history. The ideas and activism of black women in Britain tended to be subsumed within the homogenised categories of either 'black people' or 'women'. Not surprisingly, much of what is written on black women's organisations in Britain dates from the 1980s, when both the women's movement and the black movement made substantial impacts on voluntary and community organisation. Black women were to be found at the heart of both movements, and throughout the 1980s also established organisations of their own. Documentation on the roles and relationships of these organisations within the voluntary sector was sadly not completed before the funding crisis of the late 1980s and early 1990s in local government, which contributed to the demise of many of early initiatives engineered by black women.

We are made aware of the survival and regeneration of some black women's organisations into the 1990s through the work of Julia Sudbury.[1] Yet information on black women's organisations, both past and present, remains limited. This study considers the current changes determining the relationship between government and the voluntary sector, and asks 'how have black women's voluntary and community organisations moved into the twenty-first century?'

The 'joined-up' politics of Britain in the first few years of the new century envisages voluntary organisations sitting in partnership, being equal decision-makers in local politics, alongside the traditional power brokers of local government and the health authorities. New statutory duties have been imposed on local government and health authorities to consult with local black and minority ethnic communities about their needs.[2] For the first time, central government has also begun the process of devising a coherent strategy with regards to the black and minority ethnic voluntary sector. According to Paul Boateng MP:

> *The government is committed to creating a society where everyone, regardless of their colour or background, has equal rights, responsibilities, opportunities, and access to services. The black and minority ethnic voluntary sector has a vital role to play in achieving our aims of a fair, more inclusive society. By empowering black and minority ethnic groups, we can work in partnership to tackle the social inclusion experienced by too many black and minority ethnic communities.[3]*

Similar sentiments about empowerment and inclusion are also to be found in the report by the ministerial group on public order and community cohesion. In its discussion on building cohesive communities, this report stipulated the need for partnership between government and local agencies alongside the development of inclusive, effective policy responses involving all sections of all local communities.[4] Even the European Union has begun to focus its attention on the black voluntary sector, commissioning two reports specifically on the position of black and migrant women in Europe.[5]

This study of black women's voluntary and community organisation is highly relevant to current social policy. In concentrating on mapping the forms, content and ideals of black women's organisations and their relationships to the state, this study seeks to inform local and central policy. It does this through raising consciousness and understanding of the possible structures and ideals that constitute this unique element of the voluntary sector.

In many ways, this is an ambitious study. Past research on black women's organisations and services has tended to be issue-specific.[6] There have also been a small number of theoretical studies that have largely concentrated on positioning black women within British society,[7] alongside analysis of the ideological foundations of black women's organisations in Britain.[8]

In common with all of the aforementioned works, this study intends to voice and give visibility to the activism and ideas of black women's organisations

and, indirectly, to the women whom they serve. It seeks to add to existing knowledge by placing at its centre the ideas and structures of black women's organisations. To this end, we begin the study of organisations by looking at the general themes of why black women organise (Chapter 2). Emphasis is placed on the principles of organisations, and the stimuli for organisation, drawing out issues concerning local and international contexts which influenced organisation. Chapter 3 concentrates on types, structures and services of black women's organisations. We also examine the relationships between black women's organisations and the state (Chapter 4), raising issues around policies, funding patterns and levels, as well as disparities between ethnic groupings.

Aims and objectives

The major aim of this study was to undertake a comparative analysis of different types of black women's voluntary and community organisations within England, Scotland and Wales. By including a range of organisations in a variety of geographical locations, we were able to compare and contrast regional differences, the roles played by different minority ethnic groups, and factors that enhance or hinder organisation.

Within this overall aim, the research also attempted to address two specific objectives. First, to explore what determines needs, types, and structures of black women's organisations. We were interested to see if black women's organisation arose out of similar or different needs, and whether the types and structures of organisations followed similar patterns according to determined needs, or whether other factors determined type and structure. To this end, we purposely selected organisations that differed in many respects, for example longevity, service provision and histories.

Second, we wanted to examine the extent to which current funding policies and arrangements reflected the stated needs and principles of black women's organisations, or if funding policies drove needs and principles. Following a similar route, we also wanted to explore the relationship between the funding policies and the development of different kinds of organisations by different communities. Do funding policies support some types of organisation more than others, and if so why? If funding policies support some types of organisation more than others, how do other types of organisations sustain themselves and the communities they serve?

Methods

Methodologically, the intersection of race and gender presented by black women, and the need to reflect their interests and standpoints, has formed the basis of this research. This study has sought to explore and analyse black women's voluntary and community organisation in terms of two key interactive poles of their experience: as women (women-centredness), and as black people (recognition of 'race' and racism).[9] By adopting this approach, we hoped to place the voices of this marginalised grouping at the centre of this study.

We recognised that no single organisation, or organisations within any one locale, could be taken to represent the breadth and depth of black women's organisations. Since it was not possible within the resources available to conduct a nationwide study of all organisations, a cross-section was selected. The sampling framework adopted sought to identify black women's organisations using the following criteria:

- All organisations in the study had to be currently operational.
- Two organisations were also selected for their longevity.
- Another two organisations were selected because they primarily reflected a mixed user group in which African–Caribbean and South Asian women were major users. Such organisations also had black women workers and management committees.
- Two women's refuges and a mental health project were selected to reflect issue-based organisation.
- A further two organisations were included to reflect refugee communities.
- One organisation that worked locally and internationally was included.
- The remaining organisations reflect specific provision for either African–Caribbean or South Asian communities.

All the above criteria were placed alongside the need to reflect a reasonably wide geographic spread in relation to patterns of black community settlement. In the final sample of core organisations, one organisation was selected from each of the following areas: Edinburgh, Liverpool, Halifax, Cardiff, Leicester and Northampton. Three organisations operated in Manchester and four are based in London. In addition to illustrating the range of black women's organisations within the voluntary sector, sampling from a wide geographical cross-section was also used to give some indication of the influence of regional and local government variations.

Fourteen organisations were selected for case studies (Appendix I), including in-depth interviews; data from annual reports, position papers and, in one case, a book on the organisation were also used. In order to understand the context within which each organisation operated, we also sought to gain a picture of other local black women's organisations and local government operating in the different areas.

The subsequent survey of local clusters of black women's organisations involved an initial search for organisations (Appendix II), and the subsequent use of questionnaires to collect more in-depth information. We distributed 48 questionnaires, of which 16 were returned by post, and 12 completed by telephone, giving a response rate of 58 per cent. We also held focus groups in three areas, bring together representatives from the organisations that served as case studies, and those from other black women's organisations in the area. Between four and six women attended each focus group meeting. Interviews were also conducted with 12 of the 13 local authorities (Appendix III), using a semi-structured questionnaire. Additional data were also collected from annual reports and mission statements, reports from statutory bodies and demographic overviews of black communities in each local authority area.

2. Why Black Women's Organisations?

Black women's organisations have existed in Britain since at least the 1960s. According to one interviewee:

In Haringey we started a group in the late 1960s called the United Black Women's Action Group. It was just a group of us who lived on a council estate who got ourselves together. We used to see each other with our young children going to school, we'd talk outside of the school, we lived on the same estate and then one thing led to the other, looking at provisions for the estate. We didn't have a tenants' place, after-school provision for the children, nothing for the children. So we started meeting in our front rooms. Some of us were from Africa, different parts of the Caribbean and we started to talk about this and by the time we knew it we'd begun to do things, getting the tenants' association started, getting the council to assist. We began to do things we never thought we'd be able to do. We got the council to allow the tenants to organise an after-school club ... and that was before they became a normal thing. [Martha]

Like the United Black Women's Action group of the 1960s, the organisations of today form around issues that adversely affect the lives of black women in Britain. Organisation is, at the very least, a means of increasing social inclusion, combating the isolating and debilitating effects of racism that can prevent black women from benefiting from mainstream service provision.

The longevity of some of today's black women's organisations makes it difficult to assess the differences between the early trail-blazing organisations and those of today. However, it is possible to identify a range of ideals that serve as a guide to why black women's organisations were established and continue to thrive.

Black political identity

Our decision to use the term 'black women' in this research took into consideration the historical political connections between women of African–Caribbean and South Asian descent. This decision is in stark contrast to its use elsewhere. The term 'black and minority ethnic' (BME) is now established within the jargon of local authorities, and used by some to make the distinction between African–Caribbean and South Asian communities. The majority of organisations which participated in this research accepted 'black' as an organisational defining category.

As an Asian women's organisation, our primary focus is Asian women. Newham Asian Women's Project [NAWP] recognises and respects the different cultural and religious identities and values of women. However, on a political and conceptual level we are part of a wider framework. At the political level, we organise collectively as women and especially as black women. For NAWP, 'Black' is a colour of resistance. It includes African, Caribbean, Asian and all other 'peoples of colour' in a political sense.[10]

The place of 'black' as a principled expression of political identity also brought to the fore an underlying commitment to anti-racism by black women's organisations. According to Liverpool Black Sisters:

The term black is used as an umbrella term in reference to all those who experience racism, both institutionalised as well as individual.[11]

Some organisations also retained an inclusive collective black political identity as a means of bypassing religious and ethnic differences:

We are not based around faith or religious and cultural identity ... we see ourselves as being different from groups like Muslim women's organisations because we do cater for all Asian women ... this is seen as a political position ... and why we would align ourselves with black feminism as a political position. [Anita]

This particular group was one of the many using the generic title 'Asian' to define the women primarily catered for by the group's services.

Another woman, who spoke of the need for Somalis to adopt a collective black identity, places a similar emphasis on bypassing what could be antagonistic differences:

Yes, here it is more stronger, and in Somali it is mainly warlords and militia, most of the grassroots they don't want fighting, but here everybody is a tribe ... differences is fought out through petty everyday issues, which makes it even more dangerous.

Different clients even among the people in the South, they fight with different tribes. So the people who fight they were coming to live here even though they know they were different from another tribe, and they have seen that I don't belong to any tribe because I don't believe it, I don't need it. What is it they need a tribe? Because they want to get protection? I don't need any protection from them. [Dhabo]

From the documentation we have received on various organisations, it is apparent that the expression of 'black' as a political principle was more overt, and used more generically, by older organisations rather than those created in contemporary times. This difference was recognised during a focus group meeting by one woman, who had been involved in black community politics since the 1980s:

In the early days, one black women's organisation would have attempted to cater for the needs of all black women, now though we tend to look to cater for our own specific group. [Ann]

Today, the names of organisations (see Appendices I and II) reflect recognition of difference within the umbrella of 'black', as projects are named for specific ethnic and religious groupings. The significance of differences within this context is difficult to judge. Certainly, the vast majority of organisations aligned themselves to 'black' as a political identity when asked. During one focus group meeting however, there was intense discussion on ownership of the term, with those regarding themselves as 'British blacks' claiming the title, almost in cultural terms, from continental Africans. The contradictions reflected in this debate were not repeated elsewhere, although the lack of communication between the organisations present at this focus group, which seemed to represent ideological differences in material terms, was reflected in other areas. Of those organisations interviewed for the study, most saw 'black' as a political principle that influenced the formation of the organisation, and the ways in which they worked.

Justice and social inclusion

Combating the injustices which evolve from the social exclusion of black women (and children) by mainstream society and within black communities was reflected in the ideas of the vast majority of organisations taking part in the study. They sought to attack fundamental barriers to social inclusion, by devising inclusive services. In their service provisions, black women's organisations dealt with structural barriers to social exclusion, and the lack of appropriate services and discriminations in service delivery in areas such as health, education, the labour market, the legal system, housing and welfare. Even the social activities provided by many of the organisations reflected the social exclusion and isolation of black women of all age groups from the increasingly individualised and culturally exclusive nature of mainstream society. In some instances, the very existence of a black women's organisation attacked a fundamental barrier to exclusion, by making black women visible.

Self-help, autonomy and empowerment

Black women's organisations strongly reflected notions of self-help, autonomy and empowerment in their ideas and literature. Expressions of independence, achievement, women-centredness, and anti-racism are the embodiment of these notions. Groups reflected the principle in a number of different ways, focusing on the self as a specific ethnic or religious grouping, black people as a whole, the individual woman, and black women as a race-gendered self. Organisations reflected the ethos of self-help and autonomy of black women through:

- their commitment to the abilities of black women and girls to think and act independently;
- the assertion of independent needs and requirements of black women, and the multiple grouping which came within the umbrella of black women;
- acknowledging and supporting the struggle of black women to define their needs for themselves.

Invariably organisations applied these principles to their specific provision.

The aim of the organisation is to help the women overcome the barriers that they face in day-to-day living, and that's done by supporting them, advice, training, and to help them really move into workshops. [Yolanda]

Black talent must be given positive expression: this society cannot afford to ignore the exceptionally rich seam of abilities that Black women and girls represent. Our role is to keep proving this point by honing the skills of women so that they can demonstrate that we can be the best at anything we choose to do.[12]

Our intention is to try and get women to have their own activities, to have their own ideas, to have somewhere where they can talk instead of telling the men everything, somewhere they can talk themselves and think about what kind of activities they need. [Dhabo]

The aim of these programmes is to empower Asian women and girls to make informed choices regarding training and employment, and to identify the steps they need to take to move forward. [Naseem]

The language in which groups express their principles, aims and objectives has changed over time. The milder, mainstream language of today's organisations contrasts starkly with radicalism of the 1970s and 1980s, as reflected in the following quotation from 1979:

Brought together by a desire to liberate ourselves from the conditions of racism, unemployment and self-destruction ... we recognise ourselves as part of a depressed black minority within an industrial state, whose ruling classes benefit from the labour of workers ... Many of us Blacks, both men and women came to believe that we were really inferior, and to some extent co-operated in our own degradation ... the co-operative principle allows us to profit together from our own labour, to strive to unify as women, and to reach towards a collective independence ... we hope to replace dependence with self-reliance, rivalry with co-operation, defeatism with confidence in our achievement.[13]

The significance of these differences will be discussed in more depth further on in this report. Now, however, we turn to the considerable similarities in principles and conditions that lead black women to organise.

The initial impetus for organisation

Irrespective of geography (and to a lesser extent political ideology) all organisations interviewed for this project spoke of the initial material impetus for organisation being in response to non-existent or inappropriate mainstream services.

The idea for the project first came into being in the early seventies. A number of local Black women came together to highlight their dissatisfaction in the provision of childcare facilities, immigration deportation controls, mental health support mechanism and the ad hoc selection and recruitment of Black foster carers.[14]

The organisation was established thirteen years ago to provide a space for Asian women to overcome their isolation and lack of access to any forms of educational, social or economic participation in society at large.[15]

There is still very little understanding and provision in both the statutory and mainstream voluntary sector for Asian women seeking help with issues that directly affect them and their families. Language barriers, officialdom and a sense of apprehension when approaching formal agencies and the general lack of appropriate support mechanisms only exacerbate Asian women's experience of violence.[16]

The combination of black political identity and women-centred principles of self-help and autonomy has provided a major impetus for black women to organise. The general reasons why black women organise are in principle very similar: accessing resources, addressing inadequacies in mainstream service provision, developing culturally specific and politically appropriate services. This is in addition to the isolation, exclusion, confusion, deprivation, oppression and sense of injustice experienced by black women who remain on the margins of British society.

For black migrant and refugee women 'state induced obstacles, racism, and lack of understanding' provide the immediate context within which they organise.[17] In addition, wider geopolitical contextual reasons, than those provided by long-standing African–Caribbean and South Asian organisations were also brought into play as part of the conditions and context under which black women seek to build organisations. To cite an African woman,

Women are among the most vulnerable groups in conflict situations ... their suffering includes displacement, loss of home and property, loss of close relatives, poverty and family separation. They are sometimes often the victims of terrorism, torture, sexual abuse and forced pregnancy ... the refugee women leave their countries to start life in a completely new environment.... The refugees' plight is compounded by having to cope in the foreign country and the ensuing cultural shock these women are suddenly confronted with. The new environment does not always offer them the means to engage in economic activities. There is constant fear, insecurity and anxiety about their children.[18]

A Somali woman echoed the sentiment of having to cope with the newness of the British environment:

The other things we do is social evenings because our clients are somewhat isolated, they are all the time at home, helping with cooking and cleaning, shopping and mainly they are single parents. And in that case you know they don't have time for a break so they need their culture. Because in this country sometimes you don't know your neighbours, and they don't talk to each other so they need time to come together, to speak to each other then they can support each other ... our intention is to combat, to break the isolation. [Dhabo]

Somali women also spoke of other ways in which relationships developed in Somalia affected the need for women to organise in Britain:

Men either they remain in Somalia and continue fighting, or they were killed, or they disappeared somewhere, either maybe in Europe but there is no communication. So our organisation helps ... search for their families. We try to make telephone communication, we spend a lot of money for telephone to contact Europe, you know to Africa, to find the husband or where the child is because some of them

they don't know where their children are. [Fatima]

The single-parent status of Somali women was said by interviewees to have been caused by the civil war but also by the ways in which Somali women and men adapt to British society.

You know the man, he has given up, back in Africa he was a breadwinner, you know he was working, she was cooking, cleaning, she was the slave of the house. But here they get entitlement by the government, the DSS they provided money, the woman she got childcare and she got income support, so she wants the man to share with the other tasks, cleaning the house, and take the child to school, so some of them they left the woman. Either the husband was killed or he ran away and we don't know where he is. [Dhabo]

All of the continental African women's organisations interviewed for this study reflected the need to understand countries from which women come, to deal with issues that migrated with the women, and those created by the nature of British society. Of the four organisations interviewed, two attempted to maintain positive links with Africa. For the women for whom the projects are devised, the links between Africa and Britain are real, and many continue to channel their experiences and understanding through them. Funding such overseas links has proved difficult for some organisations. In one case, these links have been viewed by the local authorities as beyond the funding remit of the borough.

Understanding the influence of context is an important step in the process of appreciating why black women's organisations continue to be developed in Britain today.

Local contexts: generic principles

The following examples highlight specific conditions under which individual organisations were developed. The examples also provide an insight into the importance of the principles of self-help, autonomy and empowerment, as each reflects the initial struggles within which black women engaged. We have used examples from one of the oldest black women's organisations in Britain (Black Women's Cooperative, Manchester) and a relatively new organisation (Asian Women's Resource Association, Halifax); one organisation is based in a town and the other is based in a large, inner-city area. In each case, control over the provision of services is taken, under conditions of conflict, from other power bodies. In this first example the authority from whom the women take control is the local council:

The organisation was set up in 1987 by the local authority with European Social Funding. It was initially for three months ... lasted for three years. Initially the aim was to get Asian women into the clothing industry. [Naseem]

Once European funding finished and the local authorities took on sole funding of the project, they halved the workforce but retained the previous expectations on output. Though the project flourished, funding continued to be reduced, until:

The project was given three months to wind down. We refused. At that time funding was ceased.

The project was like a guinea pig being used here and there by different mainstream organisations. When the local authorities needed to show that they were helping Asian women they funded the project. [Naseem]

For the women who took the project on and ran it without grant aid for three years, the reasons for starting an independent Asian women's project were clear.

The team that came together brought skills and experience that was geared towards Asian women and showed people in the community that certain things were possible. The people who used the scheme gave the project the recognition. They were the proof of the pudding. It was from this that the philosophy developed that the project was going to continue as a group for the women of the community.... We wanted to have a voice to talk back to the local authority to say this is right and that is wrong. This is when the whole political game started. [Naseem]

Between 1995 and 1998 the organisation ran on a volunteer basis with no paid workers.

> All we had was the management commit-tee, the women of the community and the ex-workers ... who decided to build it from scratch. [Naseem]

In contrast to the above organisation, one of the oldest black women's organ-isations in England sought to determine the development of services for black women by breaking away from the male-dominated structures of a generic black community organisation. The initial women's group had been formed to develop a skills-training programme. When the men of the wider organisation sought to control the ideology and activ-ities of the women's project, letters of suspension to all the women workers were issued and the women were locked out of the building. The women argued against this:

> The Black Women's Co-op is the only train-ing scheme that is staffed and controlled by women. It was never conceived that men would be dictating the ideology and activities ... women need to achieve success in the field of education, authority without the psychological control of men. We need to be able to stand as equals.[19]

After a series of meetings, in order to involve black women in community initiatives, it was decided that the activi-ties of the co-operative needed to be widened:

> The co-operative was also aware that the interests and concerns of Black women, although linked to those of Black men, were not the same and it was agreed that the Co-operative should show itself to be clearly autonomous and self-determining. With these objectives in mind the Co-operative decided to reform as Abasindi.[20]

The previous examples reveal that the initial context for the development of black women's organisations can evolve from conditions within which previous facilities existed. Importantly though, both examples reflect the decision by black women to determine the kind of services provided and to place black women at the centre of the decision-making process. Of the 14 organisations interviewed for the project, four evolved out of other organisations. In one case, control of the project was removed from an all-white women's management committee to black women who changed the name and philosophy of the organisation. Other interviewees, somewhat like the women of the United Black Women's Action Group, referred to above, saw a need and developed facili-ties to cater for it.

In the next chapter of this report, the forms of organisation, and types of services, highlight one of the biggest differences between ethnic groupings. In this instance, newer members to black communities have difficulty establishing and diversifying the types of services offered.

3. Types and Structures of Black Women's Organisations

Although it is possible to talk about dominant models of black women's organisation, identifying types of organisation is problematic. To begin with, though two organisations may share a similar structure, the services they provide may differ considerably. There are also organisations that are (in theory at least) oriented towards the provision of one general service area, for example mental health, media and refuge support services. Identifying functional boundaries that enable the categorisation of such organisations is less complicated than classifying the characteristics of organisations with mixed service provisions. Such organisations may carry out youth work, adult education classes, the development of social and cultural events, alongside advice and support work on the range of issues arising daily within the lives of black women.

Client groups and services

In terms of client groupings, many organisational services were divided into specific projects and age sets. Among the 14 groups interviewed for the study, 12 geared their services towards the delivery of programmes for children, young women, mothers, working women and elders. In at least three of the projects, nursery and after-school educational programmes were the most stable and consistent services offered. Similarly, five organisations had permanent programmes for elders. The Ajani African Caribbean women's centre in Leicester is a good example of an organisation that is able to divide its provision into age ranges:

> We currently have the pre-school nursery, after-school 5–12-year-olds, summer schemes, education workshops, dance and drumming. We're also widening our focus introducing extra tuition in school subjects for youth club 14–18s. Also have the BMW project (Black Man's World); it's for boys and is a joint project. Currently it's a pilot scheme to look at needs of young Black boys. The mothers asked for the project. The Nia (18–30s group) initiated the boys' project. They socialise a lot and use centre classes like Salsa but are not overtly politically active. We also have ROAR (the Real Ajani Women) more politically active and mostly in the 30-plus age group. Then there's the 'exotics' – 50-plus group; this is the strongest group in the centre. Meet three times a week, about 30 members. Attended council meetings, etc. There's also the youth club and youth forum. [Petal and Joan]

The Ajani centre was also open for drop-in advice and support, and periodically organised social and cultural events. In contrast, the African Women's Welfare Organisation, which only has a small office base, describes its work through a series of advocacy and promotional programmes as follows:

> *The female genital mutilation programme; cervical screening community health educators project; HIV awareness & prevention – Haringey; HIV awareness & prevention – Enfield; HIV prevention work with West African Communities – South London; HIV positive support project – children & families; Fit for Life – community health mentors; volunteer training project; capacity building – quality assurance project; mental health project; refugee support project.*[21]

The following programme from Newham Asian Women's Project (NAWP) is included to exemplify the possible range and depth of project work. NAWP was one of the largest organisations interviewed for the study. Although generally we would place it within the category of service provision that seeks to combat violence and abuse in the home, the services involved in such provision are very varied.

- Under the general title of **Refuge provision** NAWP has responsibility for the management of three separate refuges in Newham and of the Haringey Asian Women's Aid, which runs two refuges and an outreach centre in north London.
- **Advice work** is lead by a resource centre which hosts three specialist advice sessions per week.
- The project also has a **Training service** that provides National Vocational Qualification (NVQ) and other courses.
- **Counselling services**: crisis, medium-term and short-term operate at three different sites – the resource centre, the refuges and a GP's surgery in Newham.
- The organisation's **Youth provision** (under the general heading of *Teeen@NAWP*) is aimed at 13–19-year-olds. This project includes an 8-week programme to which users are referred from outside agencies or can self-refer. It also hosts a weekly young women's group at a local youth centre and runs workshops and discussion groups in local schools.
- **Mental health** services consist of a befriending scheme, a mental health support group and a female family therapy group. NAWP also manages the Zindaagi project to 'co-ordinate and develop specialist support services in East London boroughs for young Asian women vulnerable to suicide and self harm'.[22] This project is based within the East London and City Mental Health Trust, managed by NAWP and steered by a group of Asian women professionals in East London working directly with young Asian girls.
- Under the programme of **Children's services**, the organisation includes work within the refuge and outside it, summer play schemes, crèche

facilities, support groups and training courses.

- **Education and campaigning** programmes have various arms: anti-deportation campaigns that highlight the injustices of the one-year rule for women who want to leave their violent husbands; campaigns on behalf of women who have killed violent partners; campaigns around forced marriages. NAWP also co-manages the National Project, Imkaan, which co-ordinates policy development and networking of the Asian women's refuge movement throughout Britain.

Male client groups

Interestingly, at least five of the organisations interviewed included provisions for male client groups. In each case interviewees stressed the importance of cultivating women-centredness that did not exclude men.

The women that come to the centre usually have their sons or husbands, so although we're a women's organisation and help empower women we're also a community organisation, because we don't neglect the men in the community because they have a big part to play in the community. We know that it's harder for the women to access services than men but there are also men in the community who find it hard to access services and if we can help women to help their husbands or sons or brothers then we're all for it ... we'll help in any way that we can. [Naseem]

Five organisations had male service users; of these, one was a generic community organisation, with a women's group within it. Describing the workings of such an organisation, one respondent claimed:

There are more women involved, most of the management committee are women, most of the people who are committed to the organisation are women, most of the service users are women, and we have a lot of women volunteers. [Dhabo]

In the case of overtly women-centred organisations, the demand to service a male client group can come from female users, as in the case of the Ajani project above. As with NAWP, work with men can be viewed as part of attaining the aims and objectives of the organisation:

We increasingly recognise that the key to future success in dealing with domestic violence and the attitudes that perpetuate it, is in the re-education of the community. There is a huge potential for working with young people in schools ... we see a profound need to work with children, particularly with boys, to encourage them to engage with issues of gender equality and human rights.[23]

We even found an organisation that had been created by women in their role as mothers, 'Black Mothers Against Violence', whose focus was to work with and on behalf of young men. These groups reveal the difficulty of totally separating work with women from the needs of men, particularly young men, who as sons, husbands, fathers and brothers remain central to women's lives.

Structures of organisation

The structures of organisations featured as case studies in this study fall into two broad categories. Firstly there is the 'generic' structure, in which a core centre-based team is responsible for the creation, development and running of activities. In this model all activities are essentially coterminous parts of the one project. In contrast, the second category, which we have termed the 'projects' model, is composed of different projects, each hosting a range of activities. In this model, though individual projects are to some extent coterminous with the central project, they are also distinct projects with the ability (in theory) to be independent of the centre. Such projects are devised by workers from the central organisation (sometimes in co-operation with other organisations), and managed by it. They can be housed in premises other than that of the core organisation and their work might be integrated into the work of other larger or smaller organisations. These individual projects are often independently funded and, though they may feed from the central client group, also assist a client group that has no relation to the centre-based facilities of the main organisation.

Both models appear to require strong central organisation and leadership. The first, however, appears to be limited by the size of the premises owned by the organisation. Quite often the activities of the organisation had initially been planned, developed and based around, available premises, as had core funding. Of the 28 projects from which we obtained information, 22 said their core work was confined to one site. Of the 14 case studies, five had activities housed on multiple sites, although some projects regarded this as a weakness, while for others it was a strength. For most organisations, the size of premises limited the work possibilities and the following comment typifies this constraint.

> *The building is too small ... it's not suitable and not big enough for what we want to do. There's a lot that we want to do. We want to get into the schools; we want to extend after school into schools ... homework clubs, breakfast clubs. We need to interact a lot more.* [Joan and Petal]

In order to facilitate a wide range of activities, individual programmes or activities had to be relatively mobile as the one hall in the building has to cleared by each group. The inability to extend beyond the confines of the premises was invariably seen by groups as problematic. By some, this sentiment was expressed with much frustration as it made bringing about change extremely difficult. One worker described it as being like:

> *A hamster in cage ... knowing that there was more out there, looking for an exit, but being caught on the continual wheel*

that was the centre of its environment. [Sandhya]

The issue of limitations of premises also proved to be a major area of difference between organisations from longer-standing ethnic communities and the newer ones. Of the five organisations interviewed which geared service provision towards continental African women, only two had their own premises. The other three organisations had small rooms which they used as office space. This latter group mainly provided advice work. In the case of such organisations, a weaker, more ad hoc version of the 'projects' model is adopted, as different activities and programmes are scattered around various locations over which they have little control.

In contrast to the 'generic', centre-based model, the projects model appeared to provide higher levels of flexibility, expansion of specialism and responsiveness to the needs of users. From the fourteen case studies, three of the organisations had adapted this model in terms of current provision. Two saw the model as enabling them to provide a more comprehensive service. In some cases, a new extension project had been drafted into service areas of other organisations, thus enabling the principles, working practices, knowledge and expertise of the black women's organisations to be integrated into mainstream services as well as providing a community base from which black women could access mainstream services. Projects utilising this approach also appeared to engage with a wider range of funding sources.

Because you're not just a mental health project it means that you can bid for funding from the youth service, you can also do social education ... as a result the project isn't limited because it has all these different arms. [Anita]

There are advantages to using each of these two models, and some organisations use elements of both. In some cases, specifically those where projects have their own premises, organisations have used this as leverage to have specialist workers seconded from mainstream and other voluntary-sector organisations undertaking specific project work within their organisations. This, too, facilitated the sharing of skills and expertise and heightened interagency collaboration. Moving between models, or more specifically trying to move from one model to another, is also difficult, as the second appears, in material terms, to require a high level of management and administrative time. This is a resource that few organisations could claim to have, at least in the quantities required to build something beyond existing provisions.

4. Black Women's Organisations and the State

The thing is, we highlight situations, problems ... unless you can get funding to attack problems there's little you can do. With the city council you don't get the backup. You don't get 'we can't help you here but try ...' to find alternative ways of funding or doing the work. [Renee]

The relationship between black women and the state features high on the list of factors which cause black women to organise. This relationship also contributes to the sustainability of black women's organisations specifically, and to the voluntary sector in general.

Like the new movements of the time; alongside white women of the women's movement and black men from the black movement, black women took the radicalism of the 1980s into local government and the organisations of the voluntary sector. To the credit of those women, some of the organisations remain with us today and are included in this study. By the late 1980s though, the Conservative Government's attack on Labour-led local authorities began to take its toll, and many black women's organisations disappeared in the climate of severe cuts which pervaded the era.

Interestingly, the context within which we study black women's relationships to the state today is also one of substantial change and to some extent uncertainty. Central government has again tied up the workings of local government with a number of programmes based on indicators of policy and performance. Unlike the previous Conservative central administration which emphasised rates and the ability of local authorities to bring in budgets within an accepted level, or be rate-capped, the current administration appears to be attempting to enact change at all levels of local government. Quality-assurance indicators are institutionalised through such programmes as best value, compacts, partnership, social inclusion partnerships and other local strategic partnerships. Invariably, these have affected the relationship between local government and the voluntary sector.

In the following section we concentrate specifically on the relationship between local government and black women's organisations. Many of the latter continue to rely upon local government for their organisations' core funding. Changes in the pool of funding agencies now available to the voluntary sector, have now begun to be exploited by black women's organisations. Still, those organisations that had managed to develop their services substantively over time suggest the need for a mixture of funding agents with local government support remaining at the centre.

Local government: strategies and policies

Largely in response to quality-assurance indicators imposed by central government, most of the local authorities interviewed for this study were in the process of implementing new funding strategies to govern their relationship with the voluntary sector. All were involved in implementing new funding strategies. Many of those representing local authorities felt that this process was long overdue. One authority, for example, had just had its first major review of funding in 15 years. Others mentioned the 'fairness', 'better targeting' and 'competitive' nature of the changes in funding.

Most of the authorities consulted shared the view that voluntary organisations which had been recipients of funds from the local authority were no longer assured of funding in the future. Some local authorities spoke of having 'opened up' funding so that all interested organisations had to compete. In contrast, others spoke of identifying the black and minority ethnic voluntary sector as a distinct priority sector for funding.

In discussions, all the authorities interviewed spoke of streamlining their grant funding so that it mirrored the priorities identified by national and local strategies. It is clear in terms of these changes that the weight of existing differences, and differences in approaches between local authorities, will invariably make the process of change less streamlined and equal for some. This was especially pertinent when it came to black women's organisations. From the interviews conducted with authorities, it would appear that 'race' or what most officers preferred to discuss in reference to 'black and minority ethnic' representation, is considered a major strategic issue by all local authorities, but gender is not. This sentiment was also recognised by black women themselves.

> *In terms of women's issues it's very difficult here because it is politically not really seen as a big issue. There was an incredible rumpus when the Prince's Local Borough Forum started a Women's Forum because you know, 'Women's Forum', and even the County Council don't have a Women's Forum. They have a Gender Forum and are very clear about it being a Gender Forum. So yes in terms of issues of sexuality here it's very difficult; in terms of race it's a lot easier in terms of putting that coming through on that agenda.* [Anjona]

Few of the interviewees from black women's organisations could identify specific policies of their respective authorities with regard to black women.

> *Without knowing what the ideas of the council are ... can't say. Don't particularly think that they have one. The thing with black women. ... Councils have their own little band of people i.e. gay men and women, ethnic minorities, under-18s, 0–4-year-olds, elders, women. We could fit into ethnic minorities ... but there's not a*

*section that just says black women ...
there's the difference there ... but to them
we're separated into categories. Never put
the sections together.* [Renee]

*Recently we've started to see stuff about
ethnic minorities ... how much they are
ensuring that funding goes to those with
the label is hard to decipher. Don't know
if there is a specific policy addressing
black women. But we do get a lot of
paperwork through addressing ethnic
minorities.* [Naseem]

The failure to distinguish black women
was also reflected during the interviews
with council officials.

*There are a multitude of policies that
involve race relations. That's such a broad
question. In terms of women, we have a
women's officer who works within our
Best Value Unit who will oversee anything
and look at things specifically relating to
women's issues. In terms of having
policies about women there could be
hundreds. I should imagine, from flexible
working hours, through to money that we
give to the Lesbian and Gay Mardi-Gras.*
[Metropolitan authority 2]

Few authorities had a coherent strategy
when it came to positioning black
women's organisations. Yet council
officers were conscious and aware of the
reasons why black women organised,
and tended to cite many of the issues
raised by black women themselves. The
majority of officers recognised not only
the existence of black women's organisa-

tions, but the important roles they
played within local communities. Some
officers saw the need for such organisations as compounded by the fact that
local authorities had effectively been
drawn out of community development.
For example, one metropolitan authority
had lost six members of staff from the
unit that funded voluntary and community groups.

*When we had more members of staff we
were doing some direct community development ourselves in neighbourhoods
where we didn't actually fund community
organisations.... [Now] we are no longer
paid to do direct community development
and our role has become more strategic;
enabling communities to do things for
themselves, we are vehicles of funding
rather than providing direct services.*
[Metropolitan Authority 1]

In short, the voluntary sector was providing services cut by local authorities.
From the perspective of black women's
and other voluntary sector organisations,
this strategy has effectively withdrawn a
layer of support and advice. For a
number of the authorities placed in this
position, the vacuum left was to be filled
by the local Councils for Voluntary
Services (CVS), who were now expected to
be at the centre of providing information
on sources of funding, capacity-building
and sustainability of organisations. All of
these factors were said by officers to be
essential in successful applications for
funding and for the success of voluntary
organisations.

Funding patterns

The number of black women's organisations funded by local authorities ranged from zero in some to areas, five or six in others. Some black women's organisations were in receipt of considerable amounts of funding; others received only a thousand or so pounds per annum, while some received no funding at all. Grants ranged from one-off payments, core infrastructure grants and project funding, to service-level agreements and contract specifications. One organisation, which received one-off funding, described their relationship with the council with much frustration:

> *The Council they gave us only £3,000 and this £3,000 really we struggled for it; sometimes they give, sometimes they don't give and even when they give us, they give us a hard time. Ask more questions, you know they take more time than the money they are giving, because I am always writing reports for them, and they are asking that I need finance.... Even though they don't give money still they are asking me my expenditure, my income, and when I give them the income and expenditure they ask me to put in my annual report, financial account, then I have to do it again, so all of this time I am booked in for them. I can assist my clients, I can do more for the clients.* [Dhabo]

The mismatch between expectations, funding levels and capacity of the organisation is also reflected in this second example, from an organisation in receipt of core funding and contract-level agreement:

> *The city council has just introduced targets. Before you just got the money and got on with it, but change in the system means that we have to meet a certain number of training outputs a year in order to retain funding. If we don't meet targets then funding gets reduced. The difficulty is that ... we are not sure how they can say we have to produce a certain amount of outputs when a project that is getting 4–5 times the money we have is given the same number of targets.* [Renee]

In the absence of clear policies or strategies specifically relating to black women's organisations it is difficult to say why one organisation might get more funding than another. This issue was raised during interviews with representatives from Somali women's organisations in different parts of the country. There was speculation and some resentment about why some organisations received more funding than others. While we found no specific official policies devised by local authorities that could explain the distribution of funds between black women's organisations, we did find certain patterns of funding. There was little and often no core funding for migrant, refugee, faith and specific ethnic groupings. There was a notable absence of funding for specific types of services for African–Caribbean women. These two 'funding gaps' are examined below in more detail.

Funding refugee and migrant organisations

Each local authority interviewed had experienced recent arrivals of refugees from different parts of the world. All referred to their attempts to address the needs of these groups and refugees were seen as a priority for funding by several local authorities. Two local authorities interviewed had specially dedicated officers and in one case a team to work with a specific refugee group. However, funding to these groups was mainly in terms of generic provision, that is for the whole community and less often specifically for women. Some officers believed that, as the new communities became more established, women's groups and organisations would begin to develop and to seek funding. As one officer commented:

> The community sustainability of the groups has changed and women have become more assertive and are more likely to put themselves into groups for support. [Metropolitan Authority 2]

The women we interviewed seemed to think that their exclusion from specific provision reflected forms of racism, rather than what was regarded as their relative inexperience:

> Look at the Migrant and Refugee Forums ... the people who are running it ... are not refugees. Even though it is a migrant organisation, the people who are running it are not. [Fatima]

Another Somali woman organiser spoke of a council officer treating the women as if they were 'not intelligent because they were too shy to speak English'. At one particular focus-group meeting the Somali women spoke of wanting to get involved and understand the local bureaucracy better, but at being overwhelmed and not having the support to guide them through it. The following quote is taken from an interview with a Somali women's organiser in London who had attempted to participate:

> What I have seen in my borough for example, you are attending a meeting, through the meeting people they divide into section, small groups and people they take points you know, what is the priority what do you think is the priority? The ethnic-minorities view was not taken, even though mention it, they say okay this is what the ethnic minority groups they want, this is want the women want to see. This is what women want to happen. At the end of the session you know they take priority vote: which one is the point of minority? So the other major people who attend the meeting they are not women from ethnic minority; so you are going to be left out.... Yes, the next day you don't have anything, where do you go, because nobody is taking your point at the end of the day. Sometimes you think why I attend, you know I spend travel costs, I spend time you see and at the end of the day my point is still not taken. [Dhabo]

The stereotyping and subsequent dismissal of refugee women by some authority bodies was unfortunately not confined to partnership and funding meetings such as those described above, and as this interviewee's experience reflect, influences other parts of local authority bureaucracy:

> *There is another organisation across from us, they are a Legal Advice Centre, so we refer clients, because we are an organisation of ethnic minority, and our letters were being undermined by other offices, like the housing, when we write a letter, 'oh this is Somali Organisation', you know they don't call us either. If we worked for next door and they write a letter, maybe they consider that letter. [Aisha]*

Somali women's organisations were not the only ones to be refused core funding. In the vast majority of the areas covered for this study, Bangladeshi Women's organisations also fared badly. Yet, from the four organisations we interviewed with the generic title 'Asian women' in their organisations' name, three spoke of the need to find ways to improve services for Bangladeshi women. While the women's organisations actively monitored difference and were conscious of ethnic groupings that may require specific services, the lack of funding and support to Bangladeshi women's groups from some local authorities does seem to indicate that such differences are not significant enough for them.

The low level of funding to women's groups within faith organisations, raised by some interviewees, is not all together separate from the issue of migrant and refugee communities, as many, like the Somali and Bangladeshi communities, are also of the Muslim faith.

> *Traditionally ... in particularly Asian organisations seen as being faith-based, the Local Authority has seen it as totally impossible to fund them. The fact that they are funding local church groups and that kind of thing ...*
>
> *These longstanding institutes traditionally have not had any funding but they do have a fairly high-profiled women's group, high-profile in that they have people that will turn up to things like Community Forums and that kind of thing.*
>
> *I think that there is tension there in terms of what they want. What they actually want is they want funding to be able to operate their services. And at one level there is no reason why they shouldn't get that funding, apart from some Local Authority officers have got it into their heads that because they are the Islamic Institute that the women's groups will de facto have to be religiously based. [Anjona]*

Absence of services for diasporic African women

The apparent absence of a wide range and specific types of service provision for African–Caribbean women raised issues that were not necessarily covered by those of migrant and refugee women. Of the 68 organisations included in the survey of local clusters, only three specifically serviced African–Caribbean women. Three local authorities gave no funding to any African–Caribbean women's organisations and three of the organisations which participated in the research spoke of no longer providing dedicated services for African–Caribbean women. This absence of funding was marked in regard to services on domestic violence and health. Only one local authority of the 13 studied funded dedicated domestic-violence provisions for African–Caribbean women, another had also funded a health project for continental African women. This was in stark contrast to the provision of both health and domestic-violence services for South Asian women.

One local authority interviewed for this study had commissioned research to gain the perspective of black women on domestic-violence service provision, but had still to develop facilities recommended in the report.[24] The research commissioned by the authority revealed that black women felt the brunt of racism and cultural differences in even the best of domestic-violence service provision. Interviewees spoke of being:

> Unable to speak to the white workers ... I don't know if they really understood what I was going through. It made me feel very isolated.[25]

That their 'blackness' separated them from other women in the refuge, and that racism was a part of refuge life, was something most interviewees expressed and saw as yet another problem they had to cope with alongside all the other traumas. One young African–Caribbean woman talks of having to cope with racism on her own and choosing to do so rather than inform the white workers.

> I can see that one woman is racist just by the way she reacts and doesn't seem to want her kids to play with mine ... I'm just watching her. I try to keep my head down. Nobody's actually mentioned that I'm black and that it may mean something to me and the way I live ... I don't eat or anything at the refuge. I just sleep there, get the kids ready in the mornings, and spend the rest of the time out.[26]

During an interview for this study, one local authority official explained the tendency to differentiate between the types of provisions funded for different groupings as follows:

> For black women, Caribbean–African women, the issue will be race first, gender second. For Asian women obviously it is different. So consensus around what the issues are for those women, which issues should they tackle, should they be race, should they be gender? For lots of black women, race is the only uniform feature if you like; how they experience issues because of their gender is going to be very different, which is probably one reason why we don't necessarily have any black women's groups in terms of African–Caribbean women's groups. [Regional authority 1]

In contrast, black women themselves regarded the divisions as implicitly racist and represented what was becoming a trend now reflected in other areas of local-authority relationships with the black voluntary sector:

> Part of that is all that kind of stereotyping what it is to be an Asian woman and what Asian women's problems are and that kind of thing, and a lot of it is particularly with Afro-Caribbean women: I think they have a real tendency to see them as white only a different colour. They aren't necessarily perceived as having a different religious need, a different cultural need, whatever; they are just seen as white but a different colour. [Anjona]

Local authorities were seen by our interviewees to think that somehow they had now assimilated African–Caribbean women. They were said to have lost focus on anti-racism, and basically tended to see things in terms of narrow definitions of culture and language differences. Culturalist and colour-blind approaches to African–Caribbean women not only ignore their cultural needs, but also effectively undermine recognition that racism remains a major obstacle in the lives of all black women, and that it must be challenged.

Levels of funding to black women's organisations

One perception shared by all officers was that of a general lack of funds available and the increasingly competitive arena of application for funding. 'Too many applications received and not enough money' was the common refrain. Given that the overall budgets available for grant aid to voluntary groups and organisations had either been reduced or remained static over recent years, this was not surprising. Of the 14 organisations interviewed for this study, nine received some form of grant aid from the local authorities, and five of this latter group spoke of being on stand-still budgets. The static nature of grant aid from the local authorities was not however the result of recent financial cutbacks. One organisation spoke of its grant having been on the same level for seven years, while another calculated that it had been at the same level for over 12 years.

> That's not so different from when I worked here in the mid-1980s. The irony of it is that you never really stand still ... the thing about so-called standing still when everything else is going forward, is that you're effectively moving back. [Maxine]

Static funding was also seen as negating real changes over time, in organisations generally, and in the roles of workers.

> Now they having to manage whatever ex-number of staff, they have to manage this building, managing this building in terms of external people coming in, operate a whole host of different services, and the money hasn't increased. And every single day you have got this kind of

(what is it?) NACRO want more black input into it, the Volunteers Bureau want more black input into it, the homelessness agencies want more black input on it, or local domestic violence forums want more black input into it. So where is that going to come from? [Anjona]

The long-term effects of static funding were also seen by some interviewees as having affected the quality of professional workers that black organisations were able to recruit. In county councils the disparity of salaries between workers in the voluntary sector employed by projects funded by external agencies and those funded by the council was stark. In one area where the project manager's post for the black women's organisation was paid £17,000 per annum, the 'Sure Start' project co-ordinator's job was being advertised at £26,000 per annum. Similar concerns were also raised during our interviews with officials from local authorities. One officer discussed the lack of black professionals in organisations that contributed, in her opinion, to the success or failure of organisations. When asked to describe whom these professionals might be she stated:

People who work for the local authority, people who have experience of applying for funding, people who know how to complete applications, people who speak English well, people who understand how local and central government works. [Regional Authority 1]

Again it is possible that a vicious circle might be working here because, according to another officer 'We find that money can lead to professionalism' (London Borough 3).

The contrast between the analysis of the difficulties black women's organisations experienced with funding which came from the organisations themselves and that which came from officers was, to say the least, interesting. For officers, the competitive nature of funding applications was frequently mentioned. Despite this being a generalised problem for all voluntary-sector organisations, some officers felt that black women's (and all BME voluntary sector) organisations suffered particularly. Reasons stated included:

- difficulty in accessing training for management committees and funding applications;
- not being in the power structure for as long as other groups;
- not getting needs recognised by 'the powers that be';
- newness or lack of maturity of black organisations, with consequent lack of experience;
- lack of 'professionals' in black organisations due to the historical nature of black employment;
- not being sufficiently familiar with the 'system' (of applying for funding);
- institutionalised racism and sexism (of grant administrators);
- the need to fit in with a local authority funding strategy;

- lack of consensus between African–Caribbean and Asian Groups.

One local authority had recently conducted a review of recent funding applications, concluding:

> Black organisations didn't score well in terms of strength and quality of their applications. [Metropolitan Borough 1]

The officer interviewed stated that the reasons for this were twofold. First, some black and minority ethnic (BME) organisations lacked capacity and experience in applying for funding. Second, this lack was caused by BME organisations being 'bogged down' in running their organisation and providing services, caused in turn by lack of staffing and resources. This appears to be a vicious circle. Another officer who described the difficulties experienced by black women's organisations being due to lack of training in applying for funding, attributed the prevention of women's participation to the timing of training sessions and lack of child care.

There were different interpretations from the officers from the black women's organisations interviewed for this study, though many of the issues raised were similar. Rather than emphasising the weaknesses of organisations, many looked to the wider context within which organisational relationships were governed by the policies and practices of local authorities. Thus, for example, irrespective of whether we were in Scotland, England or Wales, the majority of black women organisers interviewed for this study were conscious of the changing relationship between the voluntary sector and the state. The demands for funds meant that all had to become experts in grant finding from a number of different sources. At least one organisation had taken the decision to withdraw a service in order to pay for the salary of a manager to facilitate the high level of development and administrative work now required to sustain the organisation.

Appendix IV reveals that black women's organisations have not been backwards in coming forward in terms of applying to a wide range of funding agencies other than local governments. But, in addition to exploring their own capacities, black women organisers also interpreted their difficulties in terms of the funding policies and practices of local authorities themselves, through which some partnership-funding packages were accessed and which remained key providers of core funding. The instability of their relationships with local authorities appeared to exacerbate what was already a highly complex period of transformation.

Many of the criticisms tended to focus on the lack of accountability and transparency in decision-making when budgets were cut, if they stood still, and why applications were not accepted. One experienced fundraiser, whose project had been praised by a report commissioned by the council on delivery of services to black women escaping domestic violence, spoke of the lack of explanation on the part of the council for the 50 per cent cut in project funding. She also makes an important point here about the responses of the project users. When asked about the decision of the authority to cut the project's funding, her initial response was 'Pot luck'.

I can't get any good-quality engagement on it because no one wants to say that they have actually cocked up. Because I mean I keep on saying to them, why was the service cut, on what grounds was it cut – that it wasn't achieving, giving a good quality service? ... Wasn't there a community need for it? ... We still have women who come to us ... having a building like this there is real pressure from the community to continually improve on our services, even if the funding is not there, because they see us as having a quality resource and yes they have a common-sense approach that needs to be used to its maximum, but if the resources are not there the revenue support isn't there, you know it's just extremely difficult. [Anjona]

The absence of coherent reasons and explanations for funding decisions was highlighted by a number of the organisations which participated in this study. Three of them specifically accused local authorities of being myopic, sexist and racially discriminating when it came to the funding of black women's organisations. One interviewee said that she seriously thought that officers from some local authorities have a lot of difficulties in breaking away from traditional stereotypes of black women. In her view the level of grant aid from local authorities was considerably smaller than from other agencies because many officers just couldn't conceive of black women organising projects beyond a certain size.

The negative effects of racism were also recognised by a number of the council officers interviewed for this study. Interestingly, only one authority actually referred specifically to a programme to combat racism in the funding process. This particular officer, who included racism by grant administrators as an area of difficulty for black women's organisations in getting funding, spoke of the move towards 'anti-oppressive grant making principles' (Metropolitan Borough 3). This practice tries to eliminate prejudice through installing quality systems and checks to enable all applications to be dealt with in exactly the same way and time period.

The demands of fundraising were described by a number of interviewees as becoming increasingly complex. Black women's organisations found themselves being forced to change their service provisions in order to pursue funding. From the organisations we interviewed, successful reformation appears to be dependent upon finding available time, fundraising and administrative skills. When juxtaposed with the erratic funding decisions of local authorities, it is not surprising that, of the organisations we interviewed, the one which appeared to have gained a large sum of money had done so at a time when the organisation was unable to carry out many of its originally stated aims. In contrast, organisations that continually work at full capacity (e.g. refuges) and whose staff and working arrangements are not focused towards fundraising, find themselves unable to develop.

Interviewees expected local authorities to be more conscious of local contexts, rather than ignoring them or (as is or was the case with three organisations) using localism to threaten funding. In one area, funding levels for the only African–Caribbean women's organisations in the city were being threatened by a recent urban-planning housing development which facilitated the movement of a number of black families out of the inner city into new suburban estates.

5. Black Women's Organisations in Britain

Summary of findings

Sometimes it would seem that it is not a glass ceiling which is preventing Black women [my word] from fulfilling their potential but, rather, a concrete wall. However, the work of the organisations studied here indicate that cracks are starting to appear.[27]

From the evidence gathered by this study it is apparent that black women's organisations in Britain have slowly but surely been cracking holes in the walls of exclusion since at the least the late 1960s. Over time, the height and density of these walls have changed, as have the strategies and tactics of black women's organisations.

It is difficult to assess the differences between the organisations of the early phase and those of today; this difficulty is compounded by the fact that some of today's organisations were created during the phase of early development. One of the main differences we identified came in the expression of blackness. Today, recognition of differences has seen the umbrella of black political identity transformed, through the overt stating of ethnicities and religious affiliation. On the surface, this expression can appear to present marked barriers, so much so that local authorities feel it necessary to subdivide the political alliance of 'black'. Yet, of the 30 organisations asked, only five failed to include their organisations and users under the umbrella term of 'black'.

For us, the question of black political identity raised a number of important issues relating specifically to the roles and relationships of black women's organisations. The recognition of difference inherent to the development of organisations for different ethnic and religious groups reflects a move within the black women's section of the black voluntary sector to counter enforced racialisation of black people within the mainstream, and subsequent tokenism in the funding of black organisations. The relatively limited nature of funding provided to different ethnic and religious groupings by local authorities which we found reflects a need for the black voluntary sector to begin to assert and define difference politically. This may be one of the fundamental ways of challenging the restraints of covert local authority policies which penalised difference.

We also recognise the debate to be of significance in raising the profile of black women's organisations, which appeared to be invisible when it came to local government policies, and marginalised in the distribution of resources by the larger local and regional strategic funding partnerships. Thus, for example, in a large metropolitan city like Manchester, the city council provided core funding to only four organisations: of these, service provisions of three were related to domestic violence. Of the five black women's organisations which attended the Manchester focus-group meeting, knowledge of and participation in wider funding partnerships was limited.

This limited participation in and take-up of different forms of partnership-based funding was reflected throughout the country. Of the 14 case-study organisations, only two had received monies from the Single Regeneration Budget (SRB), only one had received some Health Action Zone (HAZ) funding, and two included some form of New Deal for Communities funding. No non-funded organisations had managed to tap into partnership schemes and no new organisational areas within the black women's voluntary sector had been created. While these limitations reflected weaknesses on the part of black women's organisations, they are also indications of failure by such partnerships to recognise the significant roles played by black women's organisations in the building of cohesive communities. This marginalisation of black women's organisations from key funding initiatives stands in stark contrast to how they are perceived by local government officials.

A key discovery of this study has been the tendency of local government officials to see black women's organisa-

tions as a distinctive section within the voluntary sector, servicing distinct need. The majority of officers interviewed agreed that black women's voluntary organisations enabled social inclusion and civil engagement, thus fitting into the key strategies and policies of local authorities on social inclusion and its many variants. All the officers agreed that black women's organisations provided value for money to the community and to the local authority.

They provide a service that meets the needs of that particular community, they provide it well, they are the closest to that community, they know what the community needs better than we do, and therefore we would expect them to understand the needs of women in those communities and be able to offer a service that meets their needs most effectively. [Metropolitan authority 2]

This visible value has not however served to raise the profile and positioning of this distinct sector within most of the major funding partnership programmes currently in operation. To this end, we would conclude that black women's organisations are in one sense visible, and in another invisible.

Our investigations found a sector that, despite many obstacles, continues to regenerate itself. The longevity of some of the black women's organisations interviewed for this study reflects the strength and abilities that exist within the sector. The ability to sustain organisation is influenced by different factors, including the commitment, skills and sheer tenacity of project workers and management, providing the base for sustainability. However, few interviewees from black women's organisations were complacent, and tended to concentrate discussion on, to quote, 'Funding! Funding! Funding!' as having the major influence on sustainability.

Both local authority officials and those from our case studies saw the current flux in funding relationships between the voluntary sector and the state as adversely affecting the sustainability of black women's organisations. Funding levels and general instability of funding were not seen to match material needs. Organisations spoke of an ever-increasing demand for their services on all fronts, and particularly in terms of administration and strategic liaison work. Administration work has increased, to meet the changing demands from local and (indirectly) central government. For grant aid, in addition to the strategic developmental administrative work required in applying for funding to numerous funding agencies, organisations are now required by local authorities to quantify of services.

In order to achieve quality-assurance targets set for them by central government, local authorities and other bodies are also beginning to ask some black women's organisations to comment on numerous social policy issues. In addition, most of our interviewees spoke of the work created in the process of just getting other key agencies

to do their jobs correctly. Case-study interviewees spoke of statutory and voluntary agencies passing onto them every and any subject area, as long as there was a black woman involved and irrespective of whether or not they had the relevant expertise. Thus, for example, a local hospital contacted a black women's organisation that primarily provides training and childcare facilities, to find a black woman egg donor; there was a social services department which contacted the Bengali woman manager of an Asian women's centre that has no fostering or respite-care provision, to discuss what to do with the five children of a single-parent Bengali woman while she was in hospital.

The work required to sustain relationships with external agencies was often juxtaposed with providing a wide variety of services to the core clientele, whose needs are also changing. Yet, as the range of work and workload of black women's organisations increase, core funding is either cut without due explanation or effectively stands still.

Findings and recommendations

a   The research carried out for this study found sufficient similarities between black women's organisations in their principles and service provision for this grouping to be identified as a clear section within the black voluntary sector generally and the voluntary sector as a whole.

b   Local and central government strategies, policies and practices need to reflect the pivotal positioning of black women's organisations.

c   There was resounding agreement on the need for black women's organisations to develop the capacity to engage fully with the requirement of national, regional and local partnership funding and policy-making initiatives.

d   Facilitating this engagement process across the board will require local authorities to re-examine the core funding they provide, as part of the process of acknowledging the increased roles and responsibilities of project managers who are now the central figures in fundraising and policy partnership initiatives.

e   At the level of local and regional strategic partnership schemes, positions could be structured into the membership for representatives from the black women's organisational section of the black voluntary sector.

f   At the regional and national levels, particularly in the development of an infrastructure for the black voluntary sector, facilitating the integration of black women's organisations into the decision-making process would be assisted by having an officer responsible for working with the black women's section of the black voluntary sector in each organisation.

g   The discrepancies found in local authorities' approaches to different ethnic groupings of black women indicated a need for authorities to review and subsequently clarify their understanding of the relationship between race and gender.

h   Showing a better understanding of the intersection of race and gender could also contribute to what interviewees saw to be the need to clarify and ensure that the policies and practice of local authorities reflect fair and equitable distribution of funding to all types of black women's organisations, regardless of ethnicity or religion.

i   In this respect the processes and criteria for decision-making on funding allocation to organisations need to be open and transparent.

j   The example of good practice in the funding process involved the implementation of anti-oppressive grant-making principles for grant administrators. It may also be useful for all authorities to implement this practice and to extend it to policy- and decision-makers.

k   Black migrant and refugee women were found to be the groupings most marginalised. In addition to tackling the problems inherent in migration and refugee status, they must also deal with the debilitating effects of Eurocentrism, racism and sexism of mainstream society.

l   In regard to the funding process and the organisations of 'new communities', we found no policies or practices that clearly identified how such groups move from being the recipients of small grants into the mainstream of organisations with core funding.

m   In the case of local government funding patterns, black migrant and refugee women's organisations were particularly disadvantaged.

n   Finally, we found that part of the process of raising the sustainability and visibility of black women's organisations in the voluntary sector lay with the organisations recognising themselves (in both theory and practice) as a distinct section of the black voluntary sector specifically and the voluntary sector generally.

Conclusion

Before we embarked on this study of black women's organisations in Britain, our expectations were informed by knowledge of the radicalism of previous eras and curiosity as to whether or not black women's organisations had been able to sustain and transform themselves in the post-modern context of localism, heightened individualism, and the 'professionalisation' of the voluntary sector.

The research introduced us to organisations that can, in our view, take much pride in themselves and stand as a model of the positive efforts of black communities in Britain. For those of us who do not work on the front lines of marginalised communities, it is difficult even to imagine the complexities involved in realising the grand visions of race equality, social inclusion, community cohesiveness, empowerment and self-help. Many of us do not, as yet, really even understand the realities of exclusion. Yet, these are ideals that remain at the heart of black women's

organisations, with skills, knowledge and expertise deriving from the communities within which they work. Working with black women in black women's organisations releases benefits to the family, community and to black women themselves. The individual organisations that participated in their study came in different shapes and sizes, but all of them, considering the obstacles they and their clients faced, achieved impressive results.

The research for this study took place during a period of great change for the voluntary sector as a whole. The changing relationship between the voluntary sector and the state is reflected in the types of relations we have described between black women's organisations and the local state machinery. The introduction of multiple funding agencies and the gradual displacement of local government as the single funding agency is having considerable effects on black women's organisations. In at least three areas, local government failed to fund long-term initiatives for black women. In one case funding came from the regional authority, and in another the group worked largely through the use of volunteers with funding from a charity, and through the housing of black workers from other projects in their premises. We found examples of a sector that operated on a shoestring, yet was managing to do innovative and necessary work, which even the local government admitted it could not do. In some areas organisations had developed sufficiently to co-ordinate closer relationships with the state, by either placing aspects of their work within local authority initiatives or having seconded workers from the state apparatus bring different skills and resources into their projects.

The majority of organisations were still adjusting to the changing climate which, in the case of local-authority funded projects, left them vulnerable to funding cuts. The process of adjustment for most organisations involved some level of re-evaluation of the role of project management in relation to fundraising, financial management, and to some extent social policy, as many organisers spoke of the increased workload that evolved through government and other agencies' attempts to widen consultation. Such discussions were juxtaposed with analysis of services and service provision, and the ability of the organisations to retain existing services and respond to changing needs.

In addition to forcing organisations to examine themselves, this process of re-evaluation was also creating the conditions within which organisations must examine their relationships on a local, regional and national basis. This situation was stimulated by the devolution of funding from central government to the regions, and even the creation of a regional and national infrastructure for the black voluntary sector. In the case of the Asian women's organisations, the focus outwards, beyond the boundaries of individual organisation and locale, to the national was evident in the formation of the Asian women's

domestic violence movement (Imkaan), with influence reflected in many local Asian women's projects. Such a funded organisation may also prove to be of some benefit in increasing the visibility and material position of women of African descent, whether they are from the Caribbean or continental Africa. It is difficult to assess just how much the developments in the current phase will be based on organisations' ability to access and engage with all these different levels. This is an area for further research.

In this study we have tried to make visible black women's organisations, through analysis of their ideas and structures. We have also examined the formerly under-researched area of black women and the state. In the past, much of the attention focused on black women's organisations tended to be on the ideological debates that contributed to the demise of the radical movement forwarded by the Organisation of Women of African and Asian Descent (OWAAD) in the 1980s. In shifting attention to the specific mechanism of the state, we recognise that much (though not all) of black women's organisation in Britain is in practice not totally independent. We were able to identify a number of organisations that had not sought any funding from the state. These were attached to black political organisations like the Nation of Islam, the All-African People's Revolutionary Party, and the Black Unity and Freedom Party. There was also a wide range of faith-based organisations that contained black women's organisations. Unfortunately the time and resources required to investigate such organisations were beyond the scope of this particular project.

In the face of changes brought about by the interrelationship with the state, black women's organisations have a number of difficult choices to make. There is an intersection of ideals, and even workers, between the projects of today and those of yesterday. The relationship with the state, however, appears to be pulling organisations in a number of directions. Some organisations spoke of the need to begin to 'say no' to certain types of funding, as a way of retaining organisational integrity and marrying the humanistic principles of black women's organisations with the bureaucratic demands of government-led professionalism. The organisations we spoke to were each at different stages of this process. None had chosen not to engage; some appeared to be handling it better than others, though the ability to manage the changes appeared to be related more to the availability of time and knowledge than to level of commitment. Whatever paths black women's organisations take, we hope that we have been able to show that the sector will most probably continue and flourish as there is ample organisational skill, knowledge and commitment to see it through.

Appendix I Organisations used as Case Studies

Abasindi (Manchester)

African Women's Welfare Group (North London)

Ajani African Caribbean Women & Girls Project (Leicester)

Akina Mama Wa (London-wide and Africa)

Asian Women's Resource Association (Halifax)

Camden Black Sisters (North London)

Dadihiye Somali Development Organisation (West London)

Dostiyo (Northampton)

Liverpool Black Sisters (Liverpool)

Minority Ethnic Women's Network (Wales)

Newham Asian Women's Project (East London)

Saheli (Manchester)

Saheliya (Edinburgh)

Sojourner African Caribbean Women's Refuge (Manchester)

Appendix II Organisations in the Local Clusters Survey

Affinity – Scottish Ethnic Women

African Caribbean Women's Development Centre

African Edenic Heritage Women's Group

African Women's Link

African Women's Welfare Association (Camden)

African Women's Welfare Association (Newham)

African Women's Welfare Group

Ahlus Bata Mother & Toddlers Group

Amadudu Project

Asha Women's Support Group

Ashiyana Women's Group

Asian Women's Access Group

Asian Women's Access Project

Asian Women's Cancer Support

Asian Women's Forum

Asian Women's Forum Ltd (Haringey)

Asian Women's Group

Asian Women's Self-Help Group

Association of Ogwashi-Uku Women

AWETU

Bangladeshi People & Women's Association

Bangladeshi Women's Association (Haringey)

Bangladeshi Women's Group (Cardiff)

Belgrave Baheno Women's Organisation

Bengali Women's Project

Black Association for Women Step Out

Black Mothers Against Violence

Black Women for Wages for Housework

Dosti Muslim Women's Organisation

East London Black Women's Organisation (ELBOW)

Elland Asian Women's Group

Ghar se Ghar

Granby Somali Women's Group

Henna Asian Women's Group

Hopscotch Asian Women's Centre

Hosla Asian Women's Outreach Project

Jamait Al Nissa

Kensington Asian Women's Association

Lewisham Somali Communities Association

Manchester Bangladeshi Women's Project

Mukuyu African Women's Alliance

Muslim Women's Organisation

Muslim Women's Support Group

Nari Shanghatee Asian Women's Association

Nari Kallyan Shangho

Nigerian Organisation of Women

Noor-Ul-Quran

Okpanan Women's Association

Pragati Asian Women's Group

Pragati Women's Organisation

Progressive African Women's Association

Saheli Asian Girls & Young Women's Project

Saheyli Asian Women's Friendship Group

Sangam Women's Group

Shadha Carers Support Group

Shakti Asian Women's Refuge

Sharma Women's Centre

Social Sisters
Somali Advice & Information Office
Somali Women's Group
South East London Black Women's
 Cancer Organisation
Sudanese Women's Group
Sudanese Women's Organisation

Susan Lawrence Children's Centre Asian
 Women's Group
UK East African Women & Children
 Group
West Hampstead Women's Centre
West Hampstead Women's Group
Women's Media Project

Appendix III Local Authorities Interviewed

Camden

Cardiff

Edinburgh

Haringey

Leicester

Lewisham

Liverpool

Luton

Manchester

Newham

Northamptonshire

Appendix IV Funding Bodies Supporting the 14 Case Study Organisations

African Health Forum/Health First
Allen Lane Foundation
Arts 4 Express
Association of London Government
Bank of Wales
Barclays Bank
BBC Children in Need
Breaking the Cycle
Bridge House Estate Trust Fund
Charities Aid Foundation
Churches Commission for Racial Justice
City Parochial Foundation
Comic Relief
Commission for Racial Equality – Equal
    Opportunities Commission
Community Fund
Community Foundation
Council for Voluntary Services
Creative Training Association
Corporation of London
Department for Education and
    Employment
Department of Health
Esmee Fairbairn Trust
European Commission (DG V)
European Social Fund
Foundation for Sports & Arts
Granada Foundation
Green Street Partnership
Home Office 9 European Refugee Fund
Jack Petchey Foundation
John Moore Foundation

Liverpool Hope: University College
Local government departments or
    committees:
    Central Grants Unit
    Children's Service Unit
    Community Education
    Housing
    Leisure Services
    Social Care & Health
    Social Services
    Social Work
    Strategic Development Fund
    Voluntary Sector Unit
    Youth Services
Local health authorities
London Borough Grants
National Health Service Primary Care
    Group
National Lottery Charities Board
Neighbourhood Support fund
New Deal Partnership
New Opportunities Lottery Scheme
North West Arts Board
PF Charitable Trust
Princess Diana Trust
Powerup
Regional Arts Lottery Programme
Scottish Executive
Single Regeneration Budget
Training & Enterprise Council
Tudor Trust
Welsh Church Foundation

References

1 Sudbury, J. (1998) *Other Kinds of Dreams: Black Women's Organisations and the Politics of Transformation.* London: Routledge.

2 Department of Health (1997) *The New NHS: Modern, Dependable.* London: The Stationery Office.

Local Government Association (2001) *Supporting Inclusive Communities: Lesbians, Gay Men and Local Democracy.* Middlesex: IdeA Publications.

Home Office (2001) Published on behalf of the inter-departmental working group on resourcing community capacity building, http://www.homeoffice.gov.uk.

3 Boateng, P. (2000) *Strengthening the Black and Minority Ethnic Voluntary Sector Infrastructure,* http://www.homeoffice.gov.uk.

4 Home Office (2002) *Compact, Getting it Right Together. Black and Minority Ethnic Voluntary and Community Organisations: A Code of Good Practice,* http://www.homeoffice.gov.uk.

5 Fuchs, D. (2000) in Patel, J., 'Preface'. *Overcoming Discrimination: Selected Strategies Empowering Black, Ethnic Minority and Migrant Women.* The European Women's Lobby (EWL), http://www.womenlobby.org.

6 Mama, A. (1993) (2nd edn) *The Hidden Struggle: Statutory and Voluntary Sector Responses to Violence against Black Women in the Home.* London: London Race and Housing Research Unit.

James-Hanman, D. (1995) *The Needs and Experiences of Black and Minority Ethnic Women Experiencing Domestic Violence.* London: London Borough of Islington.

Cooke, V., S. Davis, and A. Wilson, (1999) *Domestic Violence Service Provision: Black Women's Perspectives.* Northamptonshire County Council Race Consultative Panel.

7 Wilson, A. (1978) *Finding a Voice: Asian Women in Britain.* London: Virago.

Bryan, B., S. Dadzie and S. Scafe (1985) *Heart of the Race.* London: Virago.

8 Sudbury, J. (1998) *Other Kinds of Dreams: Black Women's Organisations and the Politics of Transformation.* London: Routledge.

Sudbury, J. (2001) '(Re)constructing multiracial blackness: Women's activism, difference and collective identity in Britain'. *Ethnic and Racial Studies* 24(1): 29–49.

9 Lorde, A. (1994) 'Age, race, class and sex: women redefining difference'. In *Knowing Women: Feminism and Knowledge,* ed. H. Crowley and S. Himmelweit, Cambridge: Polity Press.

Hill-Collins, P. (1991) *Black Feminist Thought: Knowledge, Consciousness, and the Politics of Empowerment.* New York & London: Routledge.

10 Newham Asian Women's Project (2000) *Newham Asian Women's Project Summary Profile*. Newham: NAWP. (Quote from pg 1.)

11 Liverpool Black Sisters (1993) *Annual Report 1992/1993*. Liverpool: LBS.

12 Liverpool Black Sisters (1999) *Vision Statement*. Liverpool: LBS.

13 Black Women's Co-Operative (1979) *Black Women's Co-Operative Statement*. Manchester: BWC.

14 Liverpool Black Sisters (1998) *Annual Report 1997/1998*. Liverpool: LBS.

15 Asian Women's Resource Association (1999) *Annual Report 1998/1999*. Halifax: AWRA.

16 Newham Asian Women's Project (2001) *Hands Off! Annual Report 2001*. Newham: NAWP.

17 African Women's Welfare Group (2001) *Creating Opportunities/Fulfilling Potentials. Annual Report 2000/2001*. London. (Quote from pg 3.)

18 As note 17 above. (Quote from pg 3.)

19 Black Women's Co-Operative (1979) *Black Women's Co-Operative Statement*. Manchester: BWC.

20 Abasindi Co-Operative (1986) *We Were Born to Survive*. Manchester: AC. (Quote from pg 4.)

21 As note 17 above. (Quote from pg 5.)

22 Newham Asian Women's Project (2002) *Annual Report*. Newham: NAWP. (Quote from pg 73.)

23 Newham Asian Women's Project (1997) *Annual Report*. Newham: NAWP. (Quote from pg 5.)

24 Cited in Cooke et al. (note 6 above).

25 Cited in Cooke et al. (note 6 above).

26 Cited in Cooke et al. (note 6 above).

27 Patel, J. (2000) *Overcoming Discrimination: Selected Strategies Empowering Black Ethnic Minority and Migrant Women*. The European Women's Lobby, http://womenlobby.org.